Vic Brotherson is the owner of
Scarlet & Violet, nominated by
Time Out as one of London's best
specialist shops: 'This exquisite
flower shop takes your breath
away the moment you walk in the
door.' It has rapidly established
itself as one of the leading
florists in the country.

www.scarletandviolet.com

VINTAGE FLOWERS
CHOOSING
ARRANGING
DISPLAYING

VINTAGE FLOWERS
CHOOSING
ARRANGING
DISPLAYING

K Vic Brotherson

Photography by Catherine Gratwicke

CONTENTS

6   INTRODUCTION

10   ROSY & RANDOM
Natural and garden flowers; scabious, cornflower, alchemilla, hydrangea
and roses, displayed in enamel jugs, crocks, jam jars, buckets, tea cups

28   BLOSSOM & BLOUSY
Romantic, feminine flowers; off-whites, palest pinks, blush and
parchment; table layouts; flowers to wear in your hair or as corsages

54   HERBY & HOMEY
Simple arrangements in utilitarian containers; cut hyacinths, muscari,
hellebore and lavender, in greys, green whites, inky darks and lilacs

80   BLOOMS & BONKERS
Unexpected mixes of colour in retro coloured glass and kitsch jugs;
vibrant oranges, pale lilacs, blacks; dahlias, ranunculas, anemones

102   CAMELLIA & CONSTANCE
Classic flower arranging; centre pieces and grandiose settings, still
lives and specimen blooms; camellia, cherry blossom, magnolia, roses

124   HOLLY & IVY
Festive foliage and berries; reds and greens, whites and greys,
frosted and rich; garlands, wreaths, dressed candelabra and candles

152   TOOLS & RULES
The equipment cupboard; how to buy, select and condition flowers;
how to get the most for a budget; useful tips and old wives' tales

165   RESOURCES

170   INDEX

INTRODUCTION

I have been a florist since I was 21. It is all I can do and I wouldn't change it for the world. It started out as an accidental career, but looking back I guess it was an obvious choice. I grew up in the Lake District, Cumbria, surrounded by a landscape that at the time I took very much for granted (back then, I had a penchant for electric blue mascara rather than hill walking!). My mum filled our house with pattern, texture and food, passing on her love for fabrics and appreciation of colour and beautiful objects. My dad had his own business; he clearly instilled a work ethic I have been unable to shake off. I studied Fine Art and knowing that I could never make a living out of painting alone, floristry seemed like the perfect job, it felt familiar. Now after nearly 20 years of hard graft, I have started to appreciate all I have gained along the way and this book is the result of all of that.

I learnt how to 'draw' with flowers (the technical anatomy) and then how to tailor them, design them, line them up and dome them and finally how to 'paint' with them. This allows the flowers to do the work, using the colour, shape and texture to create still lives, each bunch a mini work of art, a bundle of your favourite things, a representation of your taste.

One of the biggest problems I face in my job is that I have little self-control. I like too much, my taste is varied. I love the blousy high summer bouquets, brimming with colour, but I also adore the simplicity of all-green arrangements or a single stem in a glass jar. This can make decision-making difficult for me, even after all this time working to budgets in all kinds of interiors for a huge variety of clients. A few flowers pass me by. They tend to be the ones that never die, that don't perform (like the tropicals or gerbera daisies), but I am completely blown away by all the leading ladies, the show-offs that make my life so easy (cherry blossom, magnolia, sweet peas, peonies, hydrangeas and ranunculus). With so much choice, deciding between a single stem or an overload of colour can be challenging and I still find myself walking away from an arrangement wondering if the other option would have worked better (next time!).

One of the luxuries of working with fresh flowers is that they are already beautiful, making it hard to go wrong when it comes to displaying them. I know I am lucky to have a shop full of flowers, but even if your budget is tiny and your flower choices are limited it is always possible to create something beautiful, especially if you have the right container.

When I first started out, I used to dream of having a cupboard full of vases, jugs, bottles and pots to display my flowers. Now I am lucky enough to have a shop stuffed from floor to ceiling with every conceivable shape and size of container, and yet there are still days when we need one just a bit wider or lower. My advice would be to keep as many different styles of container as possible, then your choice will be easier. My personal style is for the vintage, classic shapes of container with traditional lines that really allow the flowers to work their magic. Cornflowers in enamel jugs, dahlias in marmalade pots, hydrangeas in pickling jars – the choice is endless. I will try to cover as many styles as possible throughout the book, but hopefully you will make your own discoveries at home and get as much satisfaction as I do when you find something that really works.

I am very, very lucky to have my job. It is the same as it would have been 50 years ago, using flowers to delight, to placate, to overwhelm, to sympathise but most importantly to look beautiful. The funny rules I carry in my head I will dispense as I go along and little tips that are peculiar to me will follow throughout the book – they are things that should be shared. I adore what I do, but sometimes I wonder whether something so incredibly personal should be said out loud. However, this isn't a rule book or a 'how to' book, it's here to inspire you – a little nudge to the senses to show a different way to choose and arrange flowers. I hope it will allow anyone to paint with flowers and to appreciate the leading ladies when they arrive on centre stage.

LET THEM BLOOM
WIDE OPEN. CHOOSE
ALL THE COLOURS THAT
YOU ARE SCARED OF
& THE SHAPES THAT
ARE TRICKY & PLAY
WITH THEM. MAKE
ROSY & RANDOM
ARRANGEMENTS THAT
WILL DANCE JOYFULLY
IN A MEDLEY OF
MULTICOLOURED JUGS,
BUCKETS & BOTTLES.

Roses portray a certain classicism and romance, but they put fear into some people if I accidentally sneak a few into a 'no roses please' bunch — as if somehow they will shout 'marry me' from between the hydrangeas and dahlias. Roses are sometimes seen as an easy option because everyone knows what they are (along with lilies and tulips). The colours, the longevity and the shape of roses makes it hard for me to create a bunch without at least one in there. Mixed with other roses they maintain their beauty but lose their singular potency; placed with other flower shapes and alongside textural greens they pop out and can be given a backdrop from which to sing. This chapter is characterised by punchy colours, the crocheted blankets and graphic floral tablecloths that have become synonymous with a style of decoration that is informal and purely aesthetic. It's a good time to use the tricky yellows, apricots and reds that were so often grouped together in the past and in these days of such good taste rarely come out of the closet.

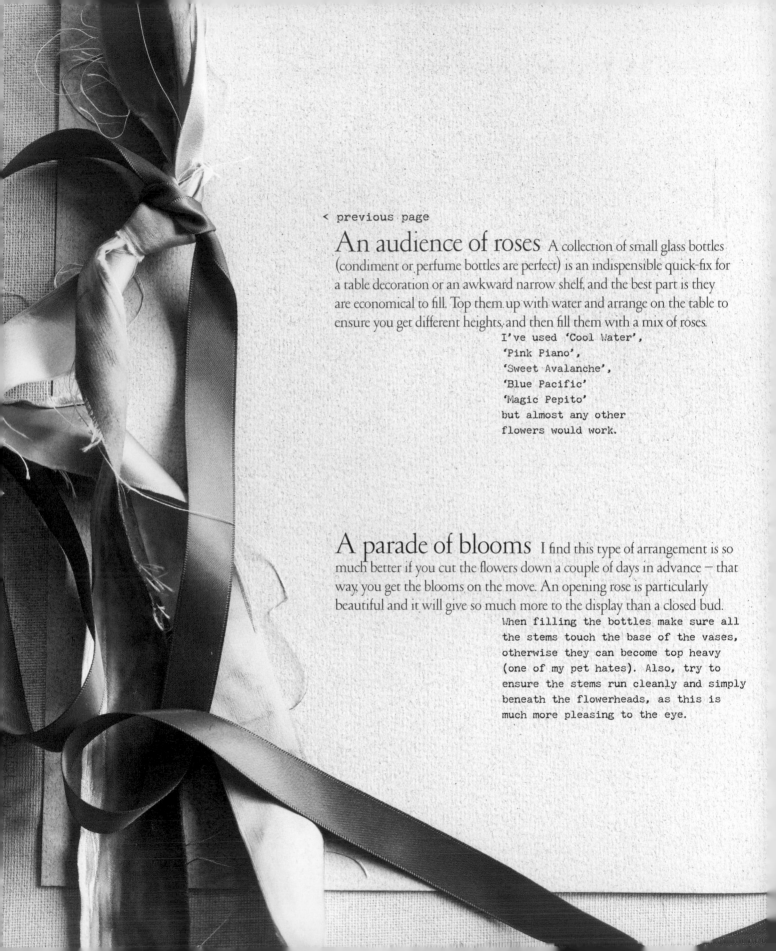

< previous page

An audience of roses
A collection of small glass bottles (condiment or perfume bottles are perfect) is an indispensible quick-fix for a table decoration or an awkward narrow shelf, and the best part is they are economical to fill. Top them up with water and arrange on the table to ensure you get different heights, and then fill them with a mix of roses.

```
I've used 'Cool Water',
'Pink Piano',
'Sweet Avalanche',
'Blue Pacific'
'Magic Pepito'
but almost any other
flowers would work.
```

A parade of blooms
I find this type of arrangement is so much better if you cut the flowers down a couple of days in advance — that way, you get the blooms on the move. An opening rose is particularly beautiful and it will give so much more to the display than a closed bud.

```
When filling the bottles make sure all
the stems touch the base of the vases,
otherwise they can become top heavy
(one of my pet hates). Also, try to
ensure the stems run cleanly and simply
beneath the flowerheads, as this is
much more pleasing to the eye.
```

ZINNIA ÉLÉGANT
DOUBLE VARIÉ

DIGITALE GLOXINOIDE
VARIÉ

VERVEINE HYBRIDE A FLEUR
D'AURICULE, VARIÉE

ADONIDE
GOUTTE DE SANG

POIS DE SENTEUR
VARIÉ

ZINNIA Élégant Double
à fleur de Dahlia, varié

Custard pot

What I find bewildering about this old slosh bucket is the fact that anyone should make something so mundane bright yellow. It is perfect for me, though, because its wide neck holds a vast amount of flowers, and I love the fact that it is ceramic rather than enamel. I started with a base of glossy, deep green camellia leaves from which I could build up the flowers. The 'Yves Piaget' (deep pink) roses are monumental in size, scent and colour but are short-lived and super fragile, so to give them the best chance of survival I propped them up using other flowers and foliage around them. The roses are dotted around the arrangement and the spaces in between filled with viburnum, lilac and flashes of orange ranunculus. A few feathery stems of Solomon's seal, which contrast with the camellia foliage, spring out around the sides to soften the edges.

ZINNIA ÉLÉGANT
DOUBLE, NAIN, VARIÉ

RICIN SANGUIN

ŒILLET D'INDE SIMPLE
LÉGION D'HONNEUR

VIOLA CORNUTA

PAQUERETTE DOUBLE
BLANCHE

< previous page, left

A high summer table

What I would give to have afternoon tea
at this table brimming with high summer
flowers. Gathered jugs and buckets are
filled with the punchiest blooms from the
shop and topped up from the garden. The
peonies are the showstoppers as the sun
pops them wide open. This yellow tree
peony has to be used whenever you can as
it has a short but magnificent season – just
one in a bottle would do for me.
Delphinium, peony, alchemilla
and allium with climbing garden
roses and mint

< previous page, right

Zesty lemon & mint

Occasional vases need not be complicated
to compliment a larger arrangement. Here,
a few individual ingredients – a handful
of herbs and a single perfect bloom – are
popped into smaller containers to set the
scene. The aim is to create a backdrop so
the eye still rests on and appreciates the
abundance of the centrepiece. Think of it
not as an individual arrangement, more as
a background display.

Porcelain roses
Sneaking a china rose in amongst the real blooms
makes you really want to touch and discover which ones are real. These Victorian
hand-painted vases are perfect for displaying unusual colours – the strong turquoise
can take the ochre and apricot, while the candiest of pinks is made even more
so with bright scarlet. The stemmed shape of these vases gives an elegance and
decadence that would have had them originally displayed as a pair on a mantelpiece,
but mismatched and placed together they make a rather more humorous couple.

Spring quartet

More often than not these jugs stand empty in their pigeonholes, but filled with flowers they bring this dark little corner to life. All diddy and easy to fill, the punchy colours are already dictated by the colourful patterns on the outside. Spring flowers tend to have short stems, making them perfect for popping into little jugs. Buy a selection of different varieties, from hyacinths and ranunculus to anemones, tulips or narcissus – a little goes a long way.

Rosy & Random 25

A painted palette An Art Deco hand-painted jug is the perfect shape for a hand-tied bunch of spring flowers. The colours reflect the graphic flower painting on the jug, but it is not a combination I would normally put together — vermillion orange carnations with blush pink ranunculus and sky blue grape hyacinths. It works because the soft, delicate shades are spaced throughout the arrangement so the eye takes in the palette as a whole, rather than being drawn to a specific colour or flower. An unusual choice, but once finished I wished I could paint and capture it.

NOSTALGIC & SWEET.
ICED GEMS, SUNDAE
DISHES & MACAROONS,
TEA CUPS & SUGAR
BOWLS, DOILIES
& TABLECLOTHS.

BLOSSOM
& BLOUSY

FEMININE & ROMANTIC,
LAYERS OF LIGHT
& LACY TEXTURE.

If you were to ask for a bunch of flowers that evoked a vintage aesthetic, this is what you would get.
The dusty pinks, blush nudes and grey lilacs, the faded but beautifully reminiscent colours of worn out satin gowns and aged lace underskirts. I think there is a seasonal aspect to these arrangements that doesn't happen in the other chapters. The feminine full heads and gentle ice cream colours seem really to be at their best in the spring and throughout the summer.
Frothy lime green or subtle grey foliage provides a lovely background and helps set off the roundness of peonies, hydrangeas and roses. This is an unashamedly girly chapter where the vases and containers are as detailed and intricate as the flowers.

Ice cream sundae

A stack of peppermint, strawberry and vanilla window vases topped off with a generous sprinkling of open rose buds. The vases are used as props to add interest and colour without adding work. The roses will keep well since they are chopped short; their heads will stay upright and open out because they are supported by the flowers around the neck of the vase. This shaped vase is a good one to use down the centre of a table as it keeps the arrangement narrow but low enough to chat over, so much more elegant than the standard alternatives. These vases were originally placed in front windows to show off the floral talent of the lady of the house. Designed to be viewed by passers by, they were a way of keeping up with the Joneses – a bit of a national pastime in those days.

A nod to nostalgia

Silk scarves and flapper girls lie alongside some French storage caddies. If flowers can evoke stories and memories in their setting they have succeeded here. Some scents transport me back to childhood and some flowers remind me of places I have lived in, and lilac always makes me feel nostalgic. It was the only beautiful thing in the garden of our flat in Maida Vale, and the scent used to drift indoors for the few days it was in season each year. Lilac is supposed to be unlucky if you bring it indoors – something about it luring in the fairies who end up playing endless pranks on the household – but the only unlucky thing I have ever experienced is its all too brief lifespan.

Here the leading ladies are the gold roses, and the supporting cast is made up of magnolias, hellebores, viburnum and, of course, the blush lilac.

My favourite jug

I have a few favourite containers, but this one is up there in my top three. It is a perfect flower jug, fat at the base with a wide enough neck to get some movement out from the vase. More than that, the pink primula pattern makes arranging the flowers a breeze. It could be filled with a few branches of camellia bud or flowering cherry and the job would be done, but, never one for the easy life, here I've filled it with hydrangeas, dahlias, roses, mimosa, snowberry and astrantia. Using two hydrangeas, or even numbers of a leading flower, has become rather a signature of our jugs and bunches. It all started because the large Dutch grown hydrangeas are so expensive, and yet I find it difficult to leave them out altogether because they are so very beautiful. Going against all flower laws (leading flowers ought always to be used in odd numbers), I gave it a go and I think it works brilliantly.

There's just one rule: the two hydrangeas need to sit at different heights in the arrangement and there needs to be a bit of movement between them, the grey mimosa and snowberry do this. Making a jug is really like creating a painting, a careful building up of layers, giving areas of rest and then intricate complicated areas of detail. Here it is provided by the astrantia, snowberry and fine delicate strands of mimosa. It is completely possible that you could build up an arrangement like this over a period of days, or even weeks, changing the flowers and the water and adding in to the existing base of greenery and longer lasting flowers.

< previous page

An old post office desk
This desk is now the resting place for a fairground horse that has enjoyed more fun-filled days. The three vases at the back have a more macabre past and were once cemetery urns. It seems strange that it is more certain we will receive flowers on our death than at any other time in our lives. Perhaps this thought will allow us to enjoy the things that are most pleasurable to us while we can. Using beautiful old vases and containers gives us a glimpse into the past, a brief moment to think of their previous life and history. The flowers we put in them are a fleeting moment that will never be exactly the same and should always be cherished.

Model's own
In the past, whenever I saw the term 'model's own' beside a photograph in a magazine you could guarantee I would end up wanting whatever it was that money couldn't buy. The expression suggests being individual, rather than following fashion. Add a flower to your hair comb, some blossom to your hat or tie a small group of wired flowers to your wrist, although I wouldn't recommend all three together.

Old crocks and gilding

These Italian pots have a crackled patina across their surface that adds character. Mixing gilded cups and saucers in amongst the heavy rustic pots ensures the table doesn't get too twee. The flowers have to work hard as they need to sweep and fall from the wide neck. As a general rule, the simpler the container the more embellished the flowers can be and vice versa.

I have filled them with elderberry, sedum and roses.

A rosy dome If you don't use a butter dish, sugar bowl, cake stand, jelly mould or even a cup and saucer, but you love the pattern, colour or shape, simply reinvent them. I'd love to use this cheese dome for its real purpose one day, but in the meantime it is way too pretty to be left on the shelf. These little roses are easy to arrange and the bonus here is the lid can house a small piece of wet foam into which the flowers can be pushed. It makes a good companion to the pretty teacups and 1940s plates.

The most coveted flower
Lily-of-the-valley has to be the most purely beautiful flower there is, with the exception of cut gardenia (which is even more elusive). The fragrance has been captured in so many scents that now we are all familiar with it, but one side of me feels we have become numb to its real beauty. To actually handle even a tiny sprig is amazing, to glimpse the delicate curve of the protective leaves and the fineness of the tiny white bells is a reminder that everything else is merely second best. It is unbelievable that such a tiny little plant could emit such a heavenly scent, it is just perfect. To capture the fragrance for as long as possible, I have planted the tiny bulbs into an old jardinière because they will last much longer on the root than as cut flowers.

Making an entrance

Hallways are the perfect place to set a mood,
even if it changes season by season. This is
a run of personal favourites – a green pickle
jar filled with blush lilac and prunus blossom,
a pair of entwined white birds, some
lily-of-the-valley in a rusty old jardinière,
the white horse, a matt pink Beswick urn
and a small carboy bottle of camellia.

A flower shrine

There are obvious places where flowers will work, but often when I put one vase down I feel compelled to go on and add more to balance out the prettiness. Left to my own devices, I have a tendency to overdo it and must try to remember it is not all about the flowers. The lilac transfer jug had been well loved when I got it, with a big chip on the foot and a gorgeous grazing across its surface. It is a proper curvaceous lady of a jug, just made for delphiniums and their grand stems.

Here, it holds couples of flowers - a pair of roses, of delphiniums and peonies - set off by spires of Jacob's ladder, along with orange blossom and waxflower to fill the gaps and tone and blend with the strong varying shapes of the leading ladies.

A tiny offering

These little cut glass vases often come in pairs, making them perfect for bedside or sofa tables. Delicate and petite, they would traditionally have been filled with garden cuttings or tiny bunches of Jersey pinks. However, I find they work perfectly as 'gesture' vases, to hold a few of the prize blooms from a larger arrangement so the eye can really savour the beauty of the individual flowers.

Dressing up

Dressing up is definitely not my forte, and I envy those who do it effortlessly. However, an occasional ostentatious bloom pinned to a dress gives such a burst of decadence and a shot of quirkiness – just enough to pick out the colour of a shoe or a piece of jewellery. Wired well, they will last for a few days as long as the embraces of the day are kept light and distant.

Silk & satin

Ladies flower corsages are seen as de rigueur for grannies and mothers-of-the-bride at weddings, but not for many others. It would be lovely to return to the days when they were worn quite regularly (I have an old photograph of three sisters in full Sunday best, each wearing a huge chrysanthemum corsage – just lovely). Roses are the obvious choice (if you're not ready for chrysanthemums or carnations yet) because they hold their shape well, providing they've had a good drink first.

These corsages are all wired. There is no reason why you need to stick to fresh flowers; here I've sneaked a porcelain rose in amongst the pink corsage and an old green silk rose in with the golden roses.

Gloria's vase This huge Constance Spry Fulham urn (in fact a pair of them) was given to me by an elderly gentleman whose wife sounds like she had huge amounts of fun arranging flowers in their home. Over the years she had amassed an extraordinary collection of vases, but these I think were surely her crowning glory. Every time I look at this vase I never feel I have done it, or indeed Gloria, justice. It has such stature alone that the flowers I put in it seem to look diminutive. Filled greedily with peonies, dill and sweet peas it takes over the mantelpiece, where only the garden foxgloves can hold their own in a painted opaline vase. Imagine a time or a place where you could have had a pair of these filled from the garden.

Pink, pink & more pink

I always think you are either a pink or a blue person. I would out loud admit to being a blue person, but then along come the candy pink hydrangeas and dahlias, the scented garden roses and the sweet peas from palest through to deep magenta pink and I drop all allegiance and stand firm in the pink territory (at least until we have cornflowers, delphiniums, scabious and muscari).

< Hunt high and low for vases and jugs that make flowers easy. Decorative and colourful containers will dictate the flowers that are used ,and narrow necks will always help with budgets. This jug reminds me of iced gems, intricately detailed and tactile it is topped with a cluster of sweet avalanche and amnesia roses, candy pink hydrangea and blush dahlia. Look at the flowers carefully and use as individual shapes and pattern when building a small detailed arrangement.

FOXGLOVE GLORY
& FEATHERY HEATHER,
A CUPBOARD FULL
OF JELLY MOULDS,
MARMALADE POTS &
DUCK EGG BLUE JUGS.
HERBY & HOMEY
COMFORTING GARDEN
GREENS. TURQUOISE
ENAMEL WASH POTS
& RICH GREEN FERNS
DOTTED WITH
SNOWBERRY, A WILD
CLIMBING ROSE & A
TRAIL OF HONEYSUCKLE.

I know I'm not supposed to have a favourite chapter but I do and it's this one. There is something about simply shaped containers and fresh, crisp colours that I find very pleasing, although it could just be that this demands the least thought from me. I love big loose branches of foliage and all the herbaceous flowers, but I have a tiny garden and no time. This chapter, then, is about arranging flowers and foliage as they would grow in nature, in an imaginary garden, allowing them to show off their leaves, the intricate detail of a petal or the subtle pigment of a stamen. Sometimes I have a moment when I see little point in what we do and wonder why we insist on chopping beautiful flowers from the ground to cut within inches of their life to put on the kitchen table. Then I remember we can only have little snippets and the vases we make indoors can only suggest the incredible ability of nature. They are but a reminder, a prompt for us to go outside and not take any of it for granted.

Stoneware & terracotta

Much like mashed potato, this arrangement is comforting and reliable. Green is always the answer when you are struggling for inspiration, as foliage gives a perfect backdrop, a familiar ground. Seasons may change, but it is always possible to create 'comfort zones' that are about solid and practical homeliness. The containers are utilitarian and the flowers and foliage are chosen for their scent, longevity and feel.

Sage & onion

play a role in a Victorian loo cistern, alongside rosemary, nigella and orange blossom, while a pair of Beswick pigs gaze nonchalantly out of the window. There are all sorts of tasty scents blended together here. The reclaimed cistern was first lined with thick plastic and filled with water, and then a hedge of rosemary was added to give the arrangement structure and some texture too. Making a big display like this one can be annoying at first because everything falls to one side (the old domino effect), but once there is enough in there it gets easier to place the flowers and keep them in position. (Be cautious if you decide to use chicken wire in a lined container as the sharp edges can rip the plastic liner and cause it to leak.)

Duck egg blue

Duck egg blue has to be the most coveted vase colour in this chapter. There is something about it that always makes an arrangement look right. These 1950s Dartmouth mantel vases (both picked up for peanuts) are filled with garden hydrangeas and pale blue scabious. I lined the bases first with a ball of chicken wire because neither of them came with their original wire frames. They are kept permanently out of the way on a cupboard top, where they become part of the decoration without taking up precious table space, and look equally good filled or unfilled.

Trifolium badium.

Monte Fcc. Sans.

ROSE CROIX

Feathery heather

Purple has always been a bit of a weird colour for me. It makes me think of religious gowns and conversely of velvet cloaked Goths, so it is carefully that I tread. There are a huge variety of beautiful purple flowers in the summer months that are impossible to ignore, however.

These show-stopping delphiniums are backed up by grasses, heather and astrantia, while the mottled pink hydrangeas are tucked in deep so they don't overwhelm.

Pots & pans

Filling pots and pans with bulbs for the New Year and throughout the spring is a brilliant, long lasting, easy and economical way to bring scent and colour indoors. I have a bit of an aversion to plastic plant pots (mum has one to plastic milk bottles on the table), so it relieves that problem too.

As the bulbs grow they can become top heavy and topple over. If this happens, one solution is to stake around the outside with birch, pussy willow or beech twigs and then you can weave the flowers back in to stand up straight.

An herbaceous entrance

A run of the most satisfyingly plump old cream
jugs filled with handfuls of garden flowering foliage.
A climbing white rose and a gentle trail of honeysuckle
is given a touch of structure with a bunch of bizarrely
shaped alliums. How nice to be welcomed home by
this drifting border. Where else are we allowed such
indulgence? The generous shapes of the jugs deserve
sumptuous filling, making this the perfect opportunity
to use greens so as not to break the bank.

Garden greens

When using foliage, make sure you strip the stems down hard of leaves so they will not be beneath the water or tangle with the other branches as they are added. Bash the base of the stems with a hammer once the height is right, or split with scissors to increase the drinking area. Let the larger branches give some height and sweep and keep the wide boughs towards the back to weight the jug. It's easy to forget to top up the water, but greens drink fast so do it daily and they should last a week or more.

< previous page left

Cupboard of joy

Shelves filled with jelly moulds and tureens have had to find a second function in my house as I am no cook. I have always loved having things on display. These lovely old things create shapes and patterns that act like wallpaper. When they are filled with odd stems the whole thing becomes a cupboard of joy — it makes me smile when I catch a glimpse of it now and again.

The flowers are aquilegia and allium and I left them in there for weeks!

< previous page right

Hydrangea tureen

What I would do without hydrangeas for a few months of the year I don't know. I have always said they are a real gift, a lazy florist's dream as they are so speedy to arrange, and when they are at the height of their season they last for ages. Hydrangeas have the most luxurious deep green leaves that serve to frame the huge indulgent flowers, so try to leave a few on around the head to give a slight relief from the potent colour — especially in the case of these electric blue ones, if only to prove they are real! Tureens and serving bowls make brilliant table centres when filled with flowers, as the sizes are already a perfect height from which to work without obscuring whoever sits opposite. It is easy to get carried away and forget that a table centre should really never be above 30cm.

MATRICAIRE
DOUBLE

Foxglove glory

This enormous Doulton pot has to be one of the most pleasurable things I have ever seen. It is huge but simple, too enormous to be filled with water so planting is a perfect solution. I would use foxgloves every day if I could — a mix of the little English ones that we can buy in bunches (like those that grow wild in Cumbria) and the large Dutch ones. Unfortunately, you can't pick the wild ones and, for the record, I have always restrained myself. Foxglove plants have such majesty and presence, I think they are at their finest left just as they are.

These are still in their pots, and they will easily outlast any cut flowers I could use — and the advantage is that they can go into the garden afterwards in the hope that my flowery fingers may one day turn green! Their season is short, but I look forward to it with relish.

Golden buttons

Great big pickling jars house the flowering bulbs of amaryllis and paper whites, the perfect containers to keep them upright and show off their humble but miraculous beginnings. Let the bulbs reach the height of the vase neck in a plant pot first, and then gently remove the soil and wash off the bulbs. Place in the jar one at a time and then add enough water to keep the roots immersed, but avoid letting the bulb stand directly in water.

A little sunshine

A container filled with one variety of flower will always look satisfying and pleasurable – as long as it's the right jug or vase, that is. Here a small stripy jug is filled with the cleanest, freshest hellebore faces, always a welcome sight in late winter.

Mop heads & buckets

An enamel bucket of hydrangeas, delphiniums and a supporting cast of waxflowers, green bells and clematis. The large, heavy-headed hydrangea sits snugly on the neck where it will drink well and be supported. An arrangement of all blues, greys, greens and lilacs was lovely, but it just lacked a shot of colour given by the 'Pink Piano' roses. Stand flower arrangements on old footstools, ladders or boxes if the surfaces aren't free of everyday clutter.

Ferns & berries

A florist's day off, a mix of all the inbetweeners creates a really harmonious show of green and white. There are no flowers as such here, just some juicy textures and shapes that play amongst themselves. A collection of jugs and vases that all work together makes the job of dressing a table an easy one. A selection of different shapes and patterns keeps the arrangement informal and the varied heights give the ferns and snowberries a good stage to perform.

The simplest palette

Considered to be the most elegant and refined combination, white and green have to be the most requested colours when it comes to flowers. However, given the option of all greens I think I would prefer it. Perhaps I have started to take lilies and roses for granted, unless it is just that leaves and textures give me a simple escape and a grateful rest from colour combining and decision making.

HOW TO MAKE A HAND-TIED BUNCH

Step 1: Select flowers that are fine in stem yet full in flower, such as hydrangea or roses, as they are much easier to handle. Rounded head shapes work together much better than a mix of rounds and spires. The magic will come with the fillers, in this case wax flower, astrantia and foliage. Chop all the stems to a manageable length (c. 30cm) and clear them of thorns, leaves and painful nodules at least 15cm from the stem base. Lay out the prepared flowers on a clear surface so they are easy to select.

Step 2: Begin by holding one of the leading flowers in your left hand and then, using your right, add from the flowers and foliage on the table. (Reverse if left-handed.) The flowers are held in place in your palm with your thumb and forefinger; the other fingers grip in and release as more flowers are added. Every third stem or so, turn the bunch using your right hand. Keep all the stems facing the same direction; as they are added the twist will become apparent. As each stem is added, slightly drop the height so as to get a lovely rounded shape.

Step 3: Finish with the hardiest stems, protecting any softer stems so that the string will not cut into and decapitate the flowers. Grasp the string around your little finger and then loop it round the bunch above your holding hand at least once. Pull tightly, place the bunch on a surface and tie in a double knot.

Step 4: Trim the stems to fit your container. Test first - you can always cut shorter! The stems should touch the base of the container and the shape of the bunch should start at the neck. It should fit snugly and not wobble.

AN ECCENTRIC
DISREGARD FOR TASTE
& SUBTLETY. A NOD
TO THE KITSCH & THE
CRAZY. BUDGERIGARS,
CANARIES, SWANS
& PARROTS. A RAINBOW
OF UNFASHIONABLE
FLOWERS,
BLOOMS
& BONKERS
A LITTLE BIT ODD &
QUIRKY, A HOTCHPOTCH
OF COLOUR, PATTERN
& TEXTURE.

Forget all you know about arranging flowers. This is a chapter that delves into the kitsch glory of dahlias, asters and carnations. There are lots of vases and containers that are considered off bounds for the day-to-day things that we do, they are site specific. I am not sure I could pop a turquoise budgie on the mantelpiece just anywhere. You need a strong constitution to sit and relax with one of these arrangements next to you. Colours have no bounds and all flowers are here to be explored — if they have been cut we may as well make good use of them. These arrangements are light-hearted and a little bit crazy, but I think it is good to let go sometimes, just to step outside the boundaries a little, although I will probably always hop back in as my love of the traditional and classic is too great.

Double chemistry

Memories of school and the story of my mum setting fire to her false nails when she was a lab technician in the 1960s spring to mind, but what stands out for me here are the turquoise and yellow bases and the simple industrial grips. Holding small old medicine bottles, each stand supports a little handful of specimen flowers that will open beautifully.

Paint pots & milk churns

This group of arrangements pushes the boundaries of traditional flower arranging by disrespecting a conventional vase and colour palette. The three containers sit close together and laugh in the face of the pretty wash jug arrangements; they are the flower bullies. The heavy-headed euphorbia with the delphiniums is perhaps the most conventional of the three, but arranged on the floor in a vast old milk churn even that flouts the rules.
The two paint pots contain a random mix of garden and Dutch flowers - snapdragons, delphiniums, green bells, dahlias and Solomon's seal. There is no respect for the odd number rule here; they are successful in their mini flower revolution.

Daisies, cows, budgies & angels

One huge collage captures all the things from my
weirdest dreams and provides an eclectic backdrop for a
bold and colourful display of vases, including a couple of
Holmegaard bottles, a pair of Victorian cobalt onion vases,
an amber decanter and a turquoise pharmacist bottle.
The daisies in the yellow jug echo the daisy pyramid in the
centre, while the crazy parrot tulips and lime fritillaries
prevent them from looking twee. Yellow chrysanthemums
stand tall and proud, not ashamed of their reputation.

Artistic licence

Magnolia is one of the great wonders of the foliage world, a cut branch of magnolia bud will open and Spring will be brought forward, even if we've rigged it slightly with the central heating. The pleasure in watching the buds open, blossom and fade is fleeting but amazing. This flock of birds started with a budgerigar and spread to parrots and doves. I am unsure of their original purpose, but I can't believe it was for flowers. Each takes a bud or two at the most. Peculiar but gorgeous, they are just the kind of odd treasures that belong in this chapter.

A huddle of swans These are still the most contentious of all the vases we use, you either love them or hate them. Too kitsch to be tasteful. Easy to fill, especially with cheap bunched flowers – in this case, asters and dahlias, but pinks, anemones or tulips would work equally well.
Just try to avoid the subtle route, it is impossible to make the swans look regal, they just look uncomfortable filled with white roses.

Wall flower A change from a painting or a mirror, a flowery heart of Icelandic poppies, lilac roses and orange ranunculus hangs on the wall. Using a foam base, it is arranged flat and then left to hang so the water can drain out before bringing it indoors. Foam bases come in many shapes and sizes (including letters and numbers) so the possibilities are endless. If you choose less fragile flowers, such as hydrangeas, statice or roses – they will dry and fade naturally without losing their beauty.

A shameless display

Carnations and chrysanthemums are banned by flower snobs, but why should anyone exclude something so accessible and inexpensive? It is ultimately down to personal choice. I know what they represent and yet I still choose to use them for their neon brightness and longevity. The whole idea of being able to whip up an arrangement from a garage forecourt tickles me and reminds me how important the right choice of vase is. This Beswick vase is perfect with its chocolate abstract pattern and elegant, classic shape.

A gentle assault to the senses

Everything about this arrangement is there for a purpose, to give aesthetic pleasure, there is no meaning or underlying story here. From the punchy fabric to the delightful little orange cyclamen jug, they are there purely for us to indulge in.

A glorious riot of colour

It is a tricky decision, all or nothing? These colours don't clash, they sit boldly next to each other — ruby, blackest red, orange and deep magenta pink. I love an oversaturation of pattern, shape and texture, but to fill every vase with every flower would detract from their individual shape and glory. When using strong colours, the eye needs some relief in order to appreciate the show-stoppers so it is more effective to keep to one variety only in a few of the vases.

Here, the small marmalade pots (one filled with roses and the other with hydrangeas) are still allowed to show off, but they don't compete with the large crock of flamboyant dahlias in the background. The containers are kept purposefully simple to allow some rest between the patterned fabric and the flowers.

Pattern & poppies A small turquoise vase
filled with Icelandic poppies and heavily scented 'Woodstock'
hyacinths is informal yet able to hold its own amid the
boldness surrounding it. Hyacinths continue growing
and flower once they have been cut. Keep them low in an
arrangement so they have room to shoot up and grab the
limelight. The papery petals of the poppies are fragile but divine
and I love their amazing spectrum of colours − from fleshy
nudes and pinks through strong oranges and neon yellows.
They often come with their protective layer intact that needs to
be gently peeled back to allow the flower to open and bloom.

Red & yellow & pink & green

orange, but not purple or blue... An old fireman's bucket is filled to explosive capacity with the finest English-grown dahlias. Whether they are embraced as kitsch or old school, dahlias have had an amazing renaissance. With us for only a few weeks in late summer, this relatively short-lived flower can be helped along if you strip the green thoroughly from the stems and keep them constantly in cool deep water – a fresh cut will also help to keep their heads held high.

CHRYSANTHEMUMS
& CORONATION CUPS,
FLOWERY MEMORABILIA.
STATELY & GRACEFUL
BOUGHS & BRANCHES,
SPECIMEN FLOWERS IN
MAGNIFIED BELL JARS.
THE NATURALIST MEETS
THE TRADITIONALIST:
CAMELLIA &
CONSTANCE
THE OLD SCHOOL
CLASSICS THAT WE CAN
FORGE & DRAW UPON.

This is the most traditional chapter in that the arrangements are inspired by the classic, elegant displays of the past. I love to scour old flower books and magazines for ideas. They are filled with often hilarious arrangements that really push the boundaries of their times. Images of carefully balanced and intricately built-up flowers staged with velvet blankets or pieces of driftwood and coral — all amazing art forms, and yet totally over-the-top by today's tastes. Nowadays we have access to a much wider variety of flowers than our predecessors, and yet back then there was a far greater understanding and appreciation of flowers, probably because many of the blooms used would have been grown in the garden of the arranger. The flowers in this chapter reflect the varieties that would have grown in a traditional English garden — hydrangeas, roses and sweet peas — with the addition of the odd rarity (slipper orchids, snake's head fritillaries, Icelandic poppies and hellebores) to make this chapter more of a curiosity.

Butterflies & sweet peas

The frothiness and gentle frill on the sweet pea stem means they are best left on their own, so as not to bruise the flower. So delicate and fragrant, sweet peas ought to be bought on the day they come in to the shop so as to enjoy every moment. Here, I have arranged them into a ball of chicken wire, building them up in layers into a big lilac and purple meringue. The black graphic shapes of these Fulham pottery vases give stature and a strong base to the flippant sweet pea. The flag iris at the back is poised ready to open. Series and groups of vases take time to collect, but they are worth the effort as they give such an easy starting point. I will generally arrange the vases first and build up the flowers and other objects as I go along.

To the manor born

When I was a lot younger, I remember thinking about living one day in the enormous house we used to visit for a garden festival. With its sweeping staircases and panelled walls covered with family portraits, it seemed quite feasible that I would live in a house like that one day! Now clearly the realisation has sunk in, it will never happen, but I suppose my job still involves elements of aspiration — especially as some of the arrangements we make evoke certain times, memories and emotions. Sometimes, subconsciously, I think I do make flowers for that stately home and then just pop them on my kitchen table, or more often than not on somebody else's. The multi-petalled chrysanthemum in this grand arrangement has a shimmering richness that makes it appear unreal, giving the impression of a dark oil painting.

The flowers were arranged into the jug starting at the base, with the hydrangea sitting close to the neck and then the wine-coloured cotinus leaves dictating height towards the back. The dusty lilac 'Memory Lane' roses blend and sit deep in the arrangement, while the golden 'Combo' rose has pride of place at the front, with one slightly further back to let the eye wander across the flowers. Finally, the wispy purple statice and white astrantia give a gentle delicacy to the dark spaces created by the foliage.

< previous page

A forgery

Arranging flowers in the classic old-school style appeals to my nature, although I find it hard to let go enough of the present day aesthetic to make arrangements quite as sculptural and contrived as they once were. Stems were often on show and space between the flowers was left bare and open; flowers were sparse and limited and I sometimes think of them as more reminiscent of Japanese ikebana, with their careful balance and proportions, rather than a country garden. I have a mixed relationship with chrysanthemums — they unwittingly turn anything made with them into a very classic arrangement. If this is the intention then they are obviously perfect, but it is rare for me to use them without first having a traditional or even ironic brief. This arrangement sits in front of a painting, the flowers are a complete forgery.

Along with the chrysanthemums, I have included wispy acer foliage, all held in place by the original wire holder that came with the vase.

The rare & the ordinary

Black slipper orchids have to be the most sinister of cut flowers. Generally, they are used with grasses and other imported orchids to create tropical extravaganzas. Unsurprisingly, I get no satisfaction from seeing them among other tropical flowers and think they should be displayed as the weirdly wonderful flowers they are against a more neutral backdrop. It is extraordinary that nature has produced something of such a bizarre texture and colour, they have a glossy stickiness that compels you to touch them. With the petrol-toned English hydrangea, they sit in an ordinary pink milk jug in an attempt to try and camouflage their peculiarity. A dense little pot of specimen flowers.

Forgotten trinkets

One February morning, I found myself in the pouring rain and pitch black at an antiques market. Foraging around I found an old condiment set and as I tentatively asked the price the seller showed me a black metal trunk filled with tarnished silver stands and hundreds of filthy unmatching little bottles. I bought the charming little bottles without a second thought. The danger of them is that they drink up the water so fast it is not uncommon for me to find a dried-up and abandoned flower on the shelf. This bottle contains one such gorgeous, forgotten rose.

Creating a quiet still life

Small groups of treasures and flowers make for peaceful little pockets. This is a time to pay attention to the smallest details, as if the flowers are part of an embroidery. Roses come in the gentlest and most nostalgic of colours. I prefer to use varieties that 'bloom wide', as watching them open, flower and then fade adds to their magic. Bell jars have an amazing way of magnifying the beauty of small flower arrangements, and are capable of turning a single rose into a tiny work of art.

Grand garden urn

Classically elegant with the
drama and detail of a Dutch
Old Master painting, this
arrangement stands beautifully
alone. The background of rich,
glossy green camellia leaves and
witch hazel branches gives the
arrangement a glory that would
otherwise be lost, the leaves
frame the delicate flowerheads
and provide a structure and line
for me to follow. It is tempting to
snip off wayward branches that
don't quite lie where you want
them, but rather than do that
try another piece. I love old
garden urns as they are a real
treat to fill but an arrangement
on this scale ought to be made
in situ (mainly because the
cast iron urn will be virtually
impossible to lift once it has been
filled with water and flowers).
Make sure you allow plenty
of space around the display to
show it off so it becomes the
decoration of the room.

The flowers are chosen
for their particular and
extraordinary beauty -
Icelandic poppies, anemones,
lilac, peony tulips,
clematis and jasmine.

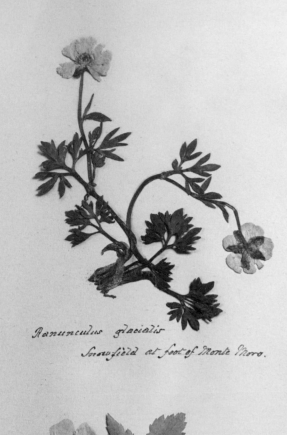

Delicate treasure
I sometimes feel a bit uncomfortable about using certain flowers. Somehow they seem too beautiful to be ripped from the ground purely for aesthetic indulgence. I console myself, probably in the same way as those who wear vintage fur, with the realisation that the deed is already done by the time I get them, and at least I can try and offer them a more pleasurable end. Snake's head fritillaries, with their delicate petals decorated with tiny little checkerboard squares, are the most detailed and exquisite flower to appear in this book and it would be unthinkable to detract from them by using any other flowers alongside. The container is crucial here, subtle enough to let the flowers be the stars, with individual glass bottles so less stems are needed. Nothing detracts from the delicate little treasures, which can dance gracefully as they drink and fade.

Ranunculus glacialis
Snowfield at foot of Monte Moro.

Ranunculus aconitifolius
Near Lausanne

Ranunculus parnassifolius
Gaden Alps.

Shy & retiring

Hellebores are the gentlest of flowers with their nodding heads that hide away the subtle blend of colours within their petals. They are the only natural winter flower that we have and are also known as Christmas roses because of this. Tricky to keep, I have tried plunging them into boiling water (the generally advised method) but cannot see it makes any difference, other than making me feel terribly guilty and giving them an awful shock. A clean, fresh cut and deep cool water seems to work just as well. I think there are some flowers that we have to accept appear for just one night only and then retire. Dressed up with a little lilac they look just captivating here.

WHEN & HOW TO USE CHICKEN WIRE

Step 1: Chicken wire should always be the first option when basic structure is needed, rather than foam, as it is reusable and the flowers are able to drink naturally. Choose a wire with large holes, about 5-8cm in diameter, as these will overlap and decrease once the wire has been folded into place. Cut a square and fold it into a cushion shape, making sure the sharp edges are twisted in to prevent them from damaging the container (watch your fingers). The size depends on the shape of your container, and is usually a case of trial and error - too much wire makes it difficult to get the flowers in, too little and it wobbles around and won't give any support.

Step 2: Place the cushion of wire into the container and fix it in place with floral tape - the best method is to tag it at four points around the very edge of the wire and fix to the rim of the container. Use as little tape as possible and try to keep it inconspicuous, otherwise you will have to conceal it with flowers and greenery as you work. If you are using wire in a clear glass container, a good trick is to line the container first with large simple leaves or a twist of trailing ivy to conceal the wire.

Step 3: Fill the container with water and add the foliage first (camellia in this urn). Try to keep the surface of the chicken wire completely free of leaves and ensure the stems are long enough to reach the base of the vase so they can drink easily. I always start by going around the rim of the container first, and then pop in some tall stems in the centre to act as a height marker. Once you have these precedents, you can then make a Mohican across the centre and again on the other side and fill the four quarters in turn.

Step 4: Once the foliage is secured in place you can start adding the flowers. Put in the leading ladies first - the hydrangeas in this case - keeping them flush with the foliage tips. You can then fill in the blank spaces afterwards with your inbetweeners (white dill in this arrangement).

RICH RED BERRIES
& GLOSSY GREEN
LEAVES, FAT JUICY
FINGERS OF BLUE PINE
& SCENTED EUCALYPTUS
& ROSEMARY.
HOLLY & IVY
WRAPPED AROUND
THE BALUSTER,
CHRISTMAS ROSES,
AMARYLLIS BULBS,
RIBBONS & MISTLETOE.
A PROMISE OF THE
YEAR TO COME.

Christmas is a time that demands all of those who celebrate it to become involved in some sort of decoration – from a tree to a table centre. Everything is brought down from the attic and the same decorations are used year in, year out. Every family has its own traditions: my mum has an amazing collection of choir singers, doves and glittery fruit that have become a family joke. It is no surprise that this has made me go the opposite way, looking to the things that are available to us naturally and evoke a real sense of the season, making and using decorations that will sit happily in the home without taking over. The making of your own decorations is something that I encourage, even if it just involves popping holly berries behind a few pictures and laying some pine on the table. There is such a wealth of bling and sparkle to choose from, it is easy to get confused. I think it is easiest to set a tone and stick with it.

A garlanded stairwell A garland
sweeps gently through two floors bringing with it the
scent of pine and an abundance and luxury that would
only be allowed at Christmas. The usually simple
hallway comes to life, bringing with it a feeling not of a
classic Christmas but a nostalgic and more subtle style
of decoration. The hanging ball of hydrangeas hovers
above the entrance, the dried out colours blending
into one another.

< previous page

A huge ball of reclaimed hydrangeas

As the season goes on, the back room at the shop fills up with hydrangea heads that have been collected from old vases. Discerningly we pluck them out of the sad bunch, tie them together and hang them from the ceiling to create a ramshackle canopy until we can reuse them at Christmas. Some hold their original colour, others are bleached out to cream and beige but all together they evoke such a beautiful hue of colours.

The ball is made from a hanging basket containing four blocks of dry foam covered with chicken wire. The hydrangeas are added until it is almost a full sphere and then it is hung up and the base filled in. The finished arrangement is surprisingly light, making it easy to hang and move around. As an alternative to dried hydrangeas, you could use fresh, but use wet foam instead to ensure they keep their colour.

Silent night
Here, a frosty midwinter palette is created using lichen, white peppercorns, Christmas roses and icy white lilac in a pewter teapot. An old silver lampbase, impossible to rewire but too beautiful to throw away, is reincarnated as a candlestick and wrapped in lichen branches simply attached with wire.

A dog's dinner

A Staffordshire dog stands guard over a simple foliage wreath filled in the centre with pots of planted hellebores to add an ironic twist. This wreath is made on a foam base, so the water can be topped up daily. There is a long list of essentials when it comes to laying the perfect table, but glass, cutlery, linen and candlelight are a good place to start. Tea lights rejuvenate a mix of old pressed glasses while the batch of old, mismatched cutlery add more character to the table once laid. The time spent lacemaking, crocheting and embroidering in the past seems beyond the majority of us nowadays, but even so that doesn't mean we shouldn't cherish them once they come into our possession.

A lacy hoop of hydrangea

The simplest of all wreaths to make in a dry foam ring, the hydrangea heads sit snugly up against each other and will last an age indoors. If the flowerheads are especially large, it might be necessary to divide them into smaller florets in order to get them to fit tightly together. Pay special attention to the edges to ensure that the plastic base is completely concealed. The trick is not to give the game away, which means hiding all your workings.

A pretty palette There is no reason to stick to the predictable white or red colours of Christmas. An old pressed glass fruit bowl is lined with trailing ivy to conceal the chicken wire cushion fixed inside, and filled with blush anemones. Next to it a celery vase is filled with astilbe that looks like tiny pink Christmas trees, and in the foreground two dinky sherry glasses hold a few heads of hellebore. To complete the scene, a small, fine garland is wrapped around the candlestick to give height and add a little splendour to the table.

A romantic wreath
Small and wintery, this romantic wreath is the girly alternative to the branches and berries that are around. A base of heather is dotted with paper roses in ballerina pink and lilac – perfect against this pale grey door.

Textural salvage A small but wonderfully tactile
arrangement of hydrangeas, white peppercorns, magnolia and silver
brunia is made into dry foam so it will last forever – or at least
until the dust becomes too much to bear! With a faded air of times
past, these flowers convey a more reflective and melancholy side to
the season and portray the skeletal branches and dried seedheads
that are part of the winter landscape. Making a small flower
arrangement is a bit like creating a mini tapestry where every space
must be filled with pattern and colour – in this case I started with
a base of hydrangeas and then added in the detail afterwards.

Goblets & urns

Scarlet red piano roses fill these etched celery vases and pressed glass goblets. Old vases add to the classic feel and the shapes are so much more elegant than any contemporary alternative. When collecting old glass vases, I find the finer etched ones to be the most beautiful, although they do tend to be more expensive. However mixed in with cheaper pressed glass, like they are here, you can get away with only one or two.

A Christmas portrait

This poor gentlemen is bedecked with a Christmas wreath and dressed all around with holly and roses, antlers and ribbon. A traditional colour scheme of red and green makes this display particularly festive. The large urn is filled with cotoneaster, autumnal eucalyptus and holly branches, the glossy red berries providing all the colour that is needed. Arranged into foam in a watertight container that drops neatly into the urn, this arrangement can be topped up to keep it fresh over the holidays (leave a small space somewhere around the back so you can fill it with water from a bottle or watering can).

Deck the halls

A door wreath, be it a crazy nest of lichen and cones or a classic twist of ivy and berries, sets the tone for the rest of your house. This wreath of rosehips and ivy conveys a traditional Christmas promise of mulled wine and figgy pudding, but a gathered bunch of greens and branches tied with a great big red ribbon would be just as inviting and a little easier to make.

With boughs of holly

The Vic Brotherson solution to Christmas at home: take the largest, simplest jug you can find and fill it with the biggest branches of holly and cotoneaster. Leave to stand against a plain wall. When you are satisfied it is as full as it can be, place a similarly simple bowl of clementines next to it and then get on with the rest of the day.

A naturalist's vase

This simple foliage arrangement would be happy on its own for a couple of weeks and the flowers could be added or taken away if the water was changed. From a distance, you get the grandness and drama of the branches; up close, the leaf shapes, fruits and lacy viburnum heads give a different pleasure. Placing an arrangement in front of a mirror will give you a tremendous sense of volume, it is a fantastic cheat to double the effect. Sweeping boughs of crab apple and cotoneaster are freshened up with limy heads of viburnum and trailing green amaranthus.

A scented introduction

A wreath made from a collection of dried and fresh ingredients gives a natural alternative to the frosty whites or reds of the season. A wreath should be chosen bearing in mind the door it will hang upon. This one is traditional in tone, but leads us to imagine the occupier might plump for the five-bird roast rather than the traditional turkey. The lavender, hydrangeas and pheasant feathers were wired in as the wreath was made, along with generous handfuls of heady scented foliage (sage, pine, rosemary and bay).

The old faithful

Dressed with a mixed bag of old and new ribbons, jam jars make a perfect run for a table centre. These dinky little hand-tied bunches consist of only the most vibrant flowers, each one slightly different from its neighbour. The jars could easily be filled with all garden greens and berries, with just the ribbon to introduce a shot of colour or a more subtle combination of whites, silver greys and parchments tied with vintage gold and silver ribbon. The leading ladies in these little bunches are the blue 'Curiosa', deep red 'Grand Prix' and coral 'Issy' roses with green bell, larkspur, statice, clematis and astrantia.

The perfect bespoke tree

Don't get me started on Christmas trees, I can see their appeal but I have opened too many Christmas tree nets and been disappointed to love them any longer. This one, however, is an exception. It is made into a bucket filled with a staked tower of wet foam, literally made to measure, with a flat back so it will sit easily in a little corner – and the most satisfying shape. Each piece of pine is stripped of needles at the base first so it can drink from the wet foam. Starting wide around the bottom, with one leading piece centrally at the top, it is a simple thing to make. Whilst using a bucket elimates the perpetual problem of the ugly Christmas tree stand.

Ho Ho Ho

The simplest windowsill arrangement, a series of old milk bottles filled with rose hips – so joyous in its speed and simplicity. There is no reason to go crazy when you can produce something so seasonal and effective.

HOW TO MAKE A GARLAND

Step 1: You will need: scissors, reel wire, ribbon or rope, blue pine, mimosa, pink peppercorns. Measure the length of the garland you would like to make using a piece of string or ribbon. Remember if you want it to festoon gently you will need to take this into account. (If the finished length of the garland is over 2m, divide it into several shorter, more manageable lengths to make it easier to hang.) I make light garlands on ribbon, but if you are going to include lots of heavy items then a fine rope (washing line) would be better. Cut the ribbon to the correct length, allowing an extra 20cm at each end to allow for hanging.

Step 2: Attach a reel of wire to the ribbon (or rope) 20cm from the end, binding it tightly to secure it. Take a small handful of foliage (here I have selected a mixture of pine, ivy and pink peppercorns) and place all the stems together to make a little bunch with the all stems facing towards you. Holding the stems against the ribbon, wrap the reel wire several times around the ribbon and stems, pulling hard to secure them. The wire will hold the foliage securely enough for you to let go and select another handful of foliage.

Step 3: Take a second bunch of foliage and position it next to the first, to cover the wires, placing it at a slightly different angle to the first so that you get a good dense cover. Without cutting the wire, bind the stems in place to secure them. Continue with overlapping bunches of foliage until you reach the end of the ribbon. Place the final bunch in the opposite direction to the others so that all your workings are hidden amongst the foliage. Cut the reel wire and twist and fix the end securely back onto the ribbon and foliage. Remember to leave 20cm of ribbon at the end for hanging the garland. Once all the foliage is in place you can hang the garland and add in all the decorative extras. The easiest way to hang a garland is to tie it in place with the ribbon.

HOW TO MAKE A WREATH

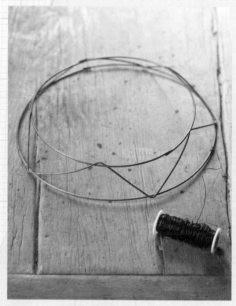

Step 1: You will need:
wire frame, scissors, reel wire,
sack moss, 5 large pieces blue pine,
4 jasmine plants. Choose a wire
frame (available from florist
suppliers), bearing in mind that
the finished wreath will end up
considerably larger than the frame
you started with. I used a 25cm
frame for this jasmine wreath and
it finished up as 45cm in diameter.
Attach a reel of wire to the
outside of the frame by looping
it around several times.

Step 2: Fill the frame with
generous handfuls of sack moss,
making sure it is damp and fresh,
packing it in tightly so that it
feels solid and dense. Take the
reel wire right the way around the
outside of the moss several times
and pull against the frame tightly
to secure it. Continue all the way
round, binding the moss in place
with the wire, until the wreath
base is complete. Turn the wreath
over and cut the wire, leaving a
little tail, and twist the end back
into the original wire frame. Cut
the foliage into 15cm lengths. Cut
the pine into 'fingers' to make it
easier to attach, discarding the
very pointy ends.

Step 3: Take a generous handful
of greenery, keeping the stems
together, and fix them into the
moss by taking the wire several
times right the way around the
base, pulling it tight to secure.
Keep the jasmine on its root to
make it last longer, wire in place
first, close to the moss, and then
place some sprigs of pine over
the top to cover the rootball and
stop it from drying out. Continue
adding foliage, paying special
attention to the outside edge to
ensure the moss is covered. Push
the final handfuls of foliage in
deep so it isn't noticeable where
the wreath starts and finishes. The
completed wreath should look bushy
and full. To keep it looking fresh,
immerse the base in water and leave
to drain before hanging, or keep
spraying it with water.

A FULLY STOCKED
CUPBOARD WITH A VASE
OF EVERY CONCEIVABLE
SHAPE. AN ENDLESS
SUPPLY OF FRESH
FLOWERS & LOTS OF
TIME. ONE DAY, MAYBE...
IN THE MEANTIME,
TOOLS & RULES
MAY HELP. TIED OR
LOOSE? WIRE OR FOAM?
ROSES OR PEONIES?

I have learnt the techniques of many people over the years, of those who I have worked for and alongside, as well as those who have worked before me. I have learnt short cuts and nifty ways to make flowers work to their full capacity and I have learnt through experimenting and through my mistakes (fortunately not too many). A lot of my decisions are based around my clients and flower choices can be derived from the individual tastes of the various people I have been lucky enough to work for and the décor of their homes that I have been fortunate enough to visit. Flowers have changed in availability during my working life, but not necessarily for the better. Today choices are endless and seasons ignored and I feel we need to get back to a more limited selection. When choosing flowers for any arrangement my rule of thumb is to go for ones that actually give me something in return and by this I mean a sense of pleasure. Whether they open and blossom, give off a divine perfume, carry an unusual shape or texture, or have an amazing colour... only then am I truly satisfied.

I have never been formally trained and learnt 'the rules' entirely through working in flower shops and from admiring and reading endless old flower books. Technicality certainly isn't my strength, but this lack has worked to my advantage and allowed me to explore ways of using flowers in a less inhibited style than I might have done had I been taught. I am not trying to create anything new through my arrangements, just something as beautiful as possible within the boundaries I am set (including availability of flowers, budget, containers, colour theme and setting). It is tricky for me to give set rules, as I know full well that for every rule I give there is bound to be an exception. It is generally my way to make things up as I go along, but that is because I have the basics instilled in my head — and probably in my fingers and scissors too — so I shall start at the beginning.

THE TOOL CUPBOARD

If you really want to be prepared for any floral eventuality then the list of tools is endless. However, if all you want to do is make the things in this book your 'tool cupboard' (or more likely your 'tools shoved under the sink') should consist of:

A good pair of flower scissors or secateurs

I have a very unladylike strength in my hands and find scissors more convenient because I can cross from foliage branches to flowers quickly. However, secateurs are easier unless you have particularly well developed hand muscles.

A small, sharp knife

The cleanest, sharpest cut is always made with a knife. A small, sharp knife is especially useful for slicing rose stems and flowers that need to drink hard (I use a knife only occasionally because it is much more time consuming than scissors).

Strong string and reel wire

This needs to be decent quality so it doesn't break when it is pulled hard against flower and foliage stems. Natural or green string works best if you are trying to disguise it, otherwise make it a feature and use ribbon or two-toned string instead.

A few blocks of floral foam

You can't reuse it and it is not very environmentally friendly, so try hard not to resort to foam too much. However, it is great when you're in a hurry and every flower arranger's dream.

A ball or sheet of chicken wire

The foam replacement, chicken wire is brilliant in vases as long as it can be disguised. Go for generous-sized holes, 2.5-5cm.

Strong floral tape

This is usually khaki green in colour and is used to hold chicken wire or foam in place (and to hold up trouser hems in my house!).

Soluble sterilisation tablets

These are a simple way to keep water clean and stop the immediate discolouration you get with natural foliage. Just be careful, though, because they act like bleach, so don't use them in precious vases or leaky jugs on valuable furniture.

CHOOSING FLOWERS

There are a million different options when it comes to containers and the same again when it comes to flowers. There are beautiful, classic and timeless blooms with texture and movement and there are ordinary modern flowers lacking either. My preference will always be for very classic flowers — roses, peonies, sweet peas, foxgloves, hydrangeas, ranunculus, anemones, and so on. However, my advice would always be to choose what you consider to be beautiful.

BUYING FRESH FLOWERS

Buy from the busy, bustly shops that have a high flower turnover (it's the old adage, never go into an empty restaurant). Alternatively, special order your flowers to ensure you get exactly what you want and when. Supermarkets carry a basic range of flowers and some do good seasonal specials, so for things like daffodils you can't go wrong.

When trying to get the longest life from cut flowers, ask your florist the following questions: 'when did these come in?' and 'how long will they last?' There are obviously no guarantees but most cut flowers will last between five and seven days. If there is no one to ask, here are a few tell-tale signs to look for yourself: check the water the flowers are stood in to see if it is fresh — if it has started to discolour that isn't a good sign; similarly, check the stems to see if they have started to soften and change colour below the water line; see if the flowers are stood relatively straight in their container — if they have started to twist and turn they are probably not as fresh as they should be. With roses, the base of the head should feel firm; with tulips and hyacinths, the flowers should be packed in tight in the leaves. If you are buying for a special occasion, make sure the flowers are going to be at their best when you need them to be — there is no point having those amazing amaryllis peaking on 23rd December. You can always control what the flowers do by moving them to a cooler/warmer room.

UNDERSTANDING COLOUR

In the shop, if a vase of yellow roses is accidentally sat alongside a jug of white stocks and a jar of pinks my heart will sink. On the other hand, if a bucket of lilac is sat beside a bunch of magnolia the day will surely be good.

When buying flowers it is easiest to set a palette and carry it through the house, this way you can always change your mind on what goes where. In many homes the backdrop is neutral, with accents of colour coming from fabric, art or flowers, and this makes the job of sticking to a colour theme much easier. Of course, colour is subjective (I struggle with red) but ultimately colour is there to be explored. My classic side will always opt for neutrals, nudes and dusky tones, or simple large branches of green or blossom, but I am also attracted by the bonkers rainbow that is all too glorious to be missed. The rule is that colours need to both tone and blend or to be completely opposite. I love transforming a predictable palette with just a little twist — an acid yellow poppy combined with orange, lilac and black and/or a deep crimson magnolia bud with an apricot rose. Finding a combination of colour that is unexpected still makes my heart leap.

HOW TO GROUP FLOWERS

Everyone I know loves peonies, so let's use them as our example. You are faced with several choices on how to group them: you can choose peonies on their own, peonies with foliage or peonies with other flowers; you can make a tight and round arrangement, or go for something more loose and blousy. To make your decision easier, I find it helps to think about the setting for your arrangement – the colours in the room, the space around the arrangement and the style or décor. If they are going on a kitchen table, a simple stoneware jug would be just fine, but peonies with a touch of personality would be so much better – a shot of lime green alchemilla mollis, a stem or two of clematis, some dill and bingo! For something less formal, perhaps to go down the centre of a table or along a mantelpiece or shelf, you could go for a selection of little glass bottles or jam jars each filled with a few stems (see page 145). If you glance around a room, there are always places where flowers would work, whether it is a small 'gesture' vase or a grand statement. One thing to bear in mind, though, if you are making more than one arrangement for a room is to go for colours that draw on each other, as this will always be much more calming.

A FEW BASIC RULES ON GROUPING FLOWERS

Flowers fall into four basic types. There are the blousy, rounded shapes – I call them the leading ladies (peonies, roses, hydrangeas, dahlias, etc.). Then we have what I call the spires, the backing singers (delphiniums, veronica, monkshood, snapdragons, larkspur, stocks, etc.). Next come the inbetweeners, the percussion (waxflower, dill, mint, astrantia, alchemilla, clematis, bluplerum, etc.). And finally we have the high season flowers, the guest stars who come and steal the limelight for a week or two (the sweet peas, scabious, etc.). Here are a few rules on which types work well together, and which combinations to avoid.

All the rounded, blousy shapes are gorgeous together; they will give a full, luxurious and classic shape.

All the rounds work with the inbetweeners; this will make for a fuller and more gardeny look and will allow the rounded shapes to show off fully while surrounded by a bit of background texture.

The spires all work with each other; they always give a more dramatic and less formal feel. Spires generally look more handpicked and less floristy than rounded blooms and they also work with texture (the inbetweeners). Spires, however, are much more difficult to mix successfully with rounds as there is a danger of what we call the 'sputnik' effect, a beautiful arrangement with antennae!

Here come the exceptions... if flowers are chosen purely for their beauty, then you can generally find a way to group them together. For example, carefully placed spires will work with rounds if they are used sparingly in a loose style – a grand group of delphiniums with one hydrangea sat low and another higher, the lines softened and broken with a careful selection of inbetweeners, a sweep of branch or a head of dill. If in doubt, I find the simplest place to start is to choose the leading flowers and work backwards.

THE PERFECT VASE

This is a tricky one. Vases, containers, jugs, buckets, urns, glass or ceramic, one large or loads of tiny... where to start? Even if you are lucky enough to be bought flowers, choosing the right container is still a decision you will have to make. My advice is to try to keep as many different water holding vessels in your home (and garden if you're lucky) as possible and this will make your decisions easier. The more you have to choose from, the more likely you are to find the right container for the purpose. I have been to houses with cupboards full of vases and have been disappointed to discover amazing bunches of flowers perched half-heartedly in glass cylinders. It breaks my heart. Of course, there is only so much you can do to make your flowers look beautiful, the rest they will do for themselves, but here are some basic rules to help you choose the perfect container:

Buy vases that are easy to use.
Never buy tall and wide as they will be impossible and expensive to fill, unless you have a garden to cut from (or host regular weddings). A classic in-and-out shape gives a narrow neck to hold the flowers in place easily. I frequently use pickle jars a or Victorian vases.

Choose vases that work in specific places around the home.
Old window vases and pairs of Victorian vases work well on mantelpieces, jugs and tumblers in groups on kitchen tables, pressed glass bud vases or patterned milk jugs on bedside tables. Try to keep a few styles for each key place to bring out at different times throughout the year when seasons will affect the height of what you choose – short, fat and full in spring, taller in summer.

The perfect container will work in its setting even if it has no flowers in it.
This basic principle should encourage you to choose vases that are a bit more interesting than a plain glass tank.

Don't be afraid to cut flowers down to sit correctly into the vase.
There is no reason why a delphinium has to stay almost a metre long; in fact, most flowers will last significantly longer if they are chopped short.

Use ceramic vases if you want to be quick
and then the stems don't need to look tidy.

PREPARING THE FLOWERS

Depending on where you buy your flowers, you may have to give them a good drink when you get them home and condition them to ensure they last as long as possible. Most flower shops will have done this boring bit for you. If not, you could always ask them to (it's a bit like asking your butcher to fillet a joint). First remove any excess foliage, especially any leaves that will sit below the water line. Next cut off the base of every stem (the amount depends on the container). Soft stems, such as tulips, anemones, hyacinths, need a neat, clean cut preferably made with a sharp knife. For woody stems, such as lilac or hydrangea, it is easier to cut them with secateurs, and then you need to bash the base of each stem with a hammer or split them with scissors to increase the drinking area. For best results, do this straight away when you get your flowers home to prevent the heads from drooping. If the flowers have been out of water for some time, make a fresh cut at the base of each stem and put them in a vase tall enough to support them whilst still wrapped in paper, so they can have a good drink and get their strength back — tulips and hydrangeas, in particular, will benefit from being wrapped up tight for an hour or two to stop their heads flopping.

HOW TO ARRANGE FLOWERS

How to actually create something lovely is a bit easier than it sounds. There are several different styles of arrangement depending on the effect you want to achieve.

Loose arrangements.

Arrange the flowers straight into the vase, cutting them to height as you go. I usually start with the greenery first and then add the rest of the flowers between the branches. This style makes for a loose and random arrangement, with flowers of different heights and plenty of space around each one to show it off to its full advantage. I find this method works well in narrow-necked jugs and larger vases. For instructions, see pages 164-5.

Hand-ties.

Hand tying a bunch of flowers, which simply means holding the bunch in one hand and adding to it with the other, makes for a more densely packed arrangement with a tighter shape. With this method, the flowers are cut to length after they have been tied together and the string can be kept in place in the vase or cut away to allow the flowers to breathe, but only if the vase isn't too wide. For instructions, see pages 78-9.

Arranging into chicken wire.

This is a great way to create more tricky shapes (for example, in very low or wide-necked vases), as it secures the first stems and allows you to be more sparing with the flowers and greenery. Good for all flowers that are heavy drinkers and for soft-stemmed summer flowers like sweet peas or anemones. For instructions, see pages 122-3.

Arranging into foam.

This is really just a big cheat. For environmental reasons we should always use chicken wire but foam is easy and secures flowers quickly, making for a speedy arrangement. Foam can be used in any vase, as long as it isn't visible. To conceal it in glass vases, line the sides with leaves. Bear in mind there are some flowers that just don't like foam, such as soft stemmed spring flowers (tulips and hyacinths). Note that when soaked it can be incredibly heavy. For instructions see pages 166-7.

Making a corsage

Keep a few florist wires of a good strong gauge for the flowers and a couple of lighter ones to use on leaves and softer flowers. The stems are cut off leaving just 1cm to wire through. The strong wire is inserted into the base making sure it is then fixed to the flower across the 1cm stem with another (lighter in weight) piece of wire. Each stem is then wrapped with green florist tape. The individual flowers can then be grouped together and the stems bound with ribbon. To cheat, don't wire the flowers just make a tiny little posy (with a flat back) and bind tightly with satin ribbon.

HOW TO MAKE A SATISFYING JUG OF FLOWERS

Step 1: You will need: scissors. Choose the right shaped jug, preferably one with a lovely curve up to the neck that will support your flowers and won't cost the earth to fill. Most enamel jugs and wash jugs will have this shape to the neck. Where possible choose foliage and flowers that will give you height, colour, texture and longevity. In this jug the spires are larkspur and molucella, the leading ladies are hydrangeas, the inbetweeners are yellow dill, the rounds are anemones and ranunculus, and the foliage is laurustinus and myrtle.

Step 2: Start with a basic bed of foliage. For a front-facing arrangement, concentrate on adding height towards the back; for a table centre, keep the taller stems towards the centre. (It makes sense to decide where you are going to put your arrangement first to avoid wasting flowers around the back.) Use interesting shaped foliage around the neck of the jug to soften the edges - five or six pieces should be sufficient. Make sure all the stems are stripped clean of leaves up to the neck of the vase so the flowers can find their way to the water easily. The stems should all reach the base of the container so they provide a sturdy scaffold upon which you can rest any shorter flowers later.

Step 3: Once you are happy with the foliage you can start introducing the flowers. Put in the leading ladies first - in this case two hydrangeas, one placed close to the neck of the vase and the other tucked in slightly higher and to one side. (If you decide to go for three leading ladies, the third one should be placed higher at the back.) For more on grouping flowers, see page 159.

Step 4: This is where the fun starts - filling in all the detail. Hold the stems up to the vase to check the height before you cut them and always err on the side of caution. When positioning the flowers, make sure you show off their best attributes. Use the spires throughout the arrangement and especially to give height and an irregular edge to the outline. Put in the inbetweeners next. The dill has a gorgeous shape and can happily stand proud of the greens. Place the anemones and ranunculus last so they sit deep in the arrangement.

HOW TO USE FLORAL FOAM PROPERLY

Step 1: Choose a piece of floral foam the right size for your container and soak it thoroughly before use. For best results, drop it into a bucket or sink full of water and allow it to sink to the bottom, which will take about a minute. Be patient and don't attempt to push it down to speed things up or it won't soak right the way through and you will end up with dry pockets. Once soaked, it is a completely different material – heavy, smooth and easy to cut like fudge.

Step 2: Cut the foam to shape using a knife and place in the container. Never be tempted to press or squidge it into place or you will compact the foam and it will crumble when you put in the flowers. For odd-shaped containers, use one large piece rather than lots of small ones because the water will have difficulty passing between them. If your container is large and you need more than one piece, keep the join below the water level so the water can keep topping up the foam. Secure in place with florist tape and fill the container with water to just below the rim. Avoid overfilling as some of the water will be squashed out when you insert the flowers.

Step 3: Prepare the foliage by stripping any leaves from the base of each stem. Add the foliage to give a dense coverage, making sure that the stems are inserted at least 5cm into the foam. Angle the stems so they don't cross over and avoid putting in too many in the same place or the foam will crack and collapse.

Step 4:

Add the flowers, starting with the largest and thickest stems — in this case, the lilac, roses and viburnum. Once you are happy with their position, you can put in the inbetweeners to fill any gaps. For more information on grouping flowers, see page 159. Before you display the arrangement, turn it round to make sure the foam is completely invisible from every angle.

RESOURCES

UK

ALFIES ANTIQUES MARKET
13-25 Church St,
London NW8
Amazing, jaw-dropping
collection of antique shops
and stalls with everything
from jewellery to taxidermy.
www.alfiesantiquesmarket.com

ALICES
86 Portobello Road,
London W11 2QD
Brilliantly stocked from
floor to ceiling with enamel
ware, jugs and a million
other things.

ARDINGLY ANTIQUES FAIR
Worth a visit with a van if
you need some furniture.
www.iacf.co.uk

BRICK LANE MARKET
Shoreditch,
London E1 6PU
Endless roadside market
on a Sunday morning.
www.visitbricklane.org

CARAVAN
3 Redchurch Street,
London E2 7DJ
A beautiful quirky shop
which leaves you wanting
to redecorate.
www.caravanstyle.com

CIRCUS
60 Chamberlayne Road,
London NW10 3JH
Constantly changing and
inspirational 19th and
20th century antiques.
www.circusantiques.co.uk

THE CLOTH SHOP
290 Portobello Road,
London W10 5TE
Vintage and new linens,
blankets and quilts.
A delight to the eyes.
www.clothshop.co.uk

COLUMBIA ROAD FLOWER MARKET
London E2 7RH
Sunday morning bustling
open-air market.

EBAY
An endless hunt for the rare
and the unusual.
www.ebay.co.uk

HOWIE AND BELLE
52 Chamberlayne Road
London NW10 3JH
All the weird and wonderful
objects and treasures in
one quirky store.
www.howieandbelle.com

KEMPTON ANTIQUE MARKET
Kempton Park Racecourse
Staines Road East
Sunbury on Thames
Middlesex
TW16 5AQ
Like IKEA for the coveters
amongst us. Take cash and
an empty car.
www.kemptonantiques.com

THE LACQUER CHEST
75 Kensington Church Street
London W8 4BG
Beautiful shop that I drive
past at least once a day and
cast an enviable glance in
the window.
www.thelacquerchest.com

LILLIE ROAD
Fulham, London SW6 7LL
A lovely few hours can be
spent nosing in and out
of the antique shops on
this road.
www.lillieroad.co.uk

NEW COVENT GARDEN MARKET
London SW8 5BH
Everything you could need
from scissors to flowers
to wires and a bucket.
www.newcoventgardenmarket.com

RAINBOW SUPPLIES
Online, easy, florist's
sundries.
www.rainbowfloristsupplies.
co.uk

NICHE
70 Chamberlayne Road,
London NW10 3JJ
Reupholstered furniture.
www.nicheantiques.co.uk

RE
Bishops Yard,
Main Street, Corbridge,
Northumberland
NE45 5LA
A brilliant shop with a
constantly changing
variety of refound and
recycled homewares and gifts.
www.re-foundobjects.com

VV ROULEAUX
Divine collection of ribbons
and trimmings.
www.vvrouleaux.com

[With the addition of every
car boot and charity shop
I have ever passed.]

AUSTRALIA

DUCK EGG BLUE
Darling Street, Balmain,
Sydney
An eclectic mix of modern
industrial and antique
accessories Penguin classic
notebooks, to quirky French
napery and cushions.
www.duckeggblue.com.au

EMPIRE VINTAGE
63 Cardigan Place,
Albert Park, Vic 3206
One-off, unusual, old,
decorative and functional
pieces.
www.empirevintage.com.au

HAVE YOU MET MISS JONES
Quirky bone china.
www.haveyoumetmissjones.
com.au

MAJOR & TOM
45 Barwon Park Road,
St Peters, NSW 2004
Have lots of furniture and
decorative objects.
www.majorandtom.com.au

PARTERRE GARDEN
33 Ocean Street,
Woollahra, NSW 2025
French provincial antiques
and collectables.
www.parterre.com.au

PEPPERGREEN ANTIQUES
The Market Place,
Berrima, NSW 2577
Rare old goods sourced
primarily from old estates
and households and frequent
buying trips to Europe and
the UK.
www.peppergreenantiques.
com.au

PROP.D
56-91 Moreland Street,
Footscray, Vic 3011
A prop hire company.
www.propd.com.au/blog

Also ROZELLE & GLEBE MARKETS
have great vintage finds,
plus amazing furniture
shops with modern chairs,
ceramics, etc.

[Thanks to Tracy Lines.]

A

acer 110-11, 112
alchemilla 20, 159
allium 22, 66, 68, 70
amaranthus 142
amaryllis 72, 73, 158
anemone 24, 25, 91, 117,
    134, 158, 162, 164
aquilegia 68, 70
aster 90, 91
astilbe 134
astrantia 36, 37, 62,
    63, 78, 108, 109, 159

B

bay 142, 143
beech 64
bell jars 115
berries 77, 140
    cotoneaster 138, 139,
        140, 141, 142
    elderberries 42
    holly 126, 138, 139
    snowberries 36, 37,
        76, 77
    in table centres 144
    in wreaths 76, 134, 140
birch 64
bluplerum 159
bottles 13-14, 16, 17,
    85, 86-7, 88, 114, 118,
    119, 146, 159
brunia 136, 137
buckets 18, 22, 74-5,
    100, 101, 147
bulbs
    amaryllis 64, 72, 73
    hyacinth 65, 98, 99
    lily-of-the-valley 44
    paper whites 72, 73
buying flowers 158

C

camellia leaves 117,
    122, 123
carnation 26, 27, 93
choosing flowers 154, 158
Christmas 124-47
    garlands 128, 134
    hydrangea ball 129, 130
    hydrangea hoop 133

table centres 144, 145
wreaths 135, 139, 140,
    142, 143
Christmas roses
    see hellebores
Christmas trees 147
chrysanthemums 86, 87,
    88, 95, 108, 109,
    110-11, 112
    for corsages 49
clematis 75, 117, 159
colour 8, 10-27, 30,
    32, 43, 49, 56, 60,
    64, 70, 75, 77,
    82-101, 112, 114, 120,
    128, 130, 134, 137,
    138, 158, 159
cones 140, 150
containers 9, 56-77, 160-1
    bell jars 115
    bottles 13-14, 16,
        17, 85, 86-7, 88, 114,
        118, 119, 146, 159
    buckets 18, 22, 74-5,
        100, 101, 147
    decanters 86, 88
    fruit bowls 134
    glasses 134
    goblets 138, 139
    jardinières 44, 45
    jars 45, 57, 72, 73,
        144, 145, 159
    jelly moulds 68, 70
    jugs 22, 24, 25, 26,
        27, 36, 37, 46, 47,
        65, 66, 67, 68, 72,
        73, 87, 88, 96, 108,
        109, 112, 113, 163,
        164-5
    milk churns 84, 85
    paint pots 84, 85
    pans 64, 65
    pots 64, 70, 71, 97
    stoneware 58, 59
    storage caddies 34-5
    teapots 130, 131
    terracotta 59
    tureens 69, 70
    urns 50, 117, 122, 123,
        138, 139
    vases 23, 32-3, 39, 40,
        45, 47, 51, 52, 53, 60,
        61, 86-7, 88, 90, 91,
        93, 106-7, 121, 138,

160, 163
cornflower 9, 53
corsages 41, 48, 49, 163
cotinus 108, 109
cotoneaster 138, 139,
    140, 141, 142
crab apple 142

D

dahlia 9, 36, 37, 52, 53,
    84, 85, 90, 91, 96,
    97, 100, 101, 159
daisy 87, 88
decanters 86, 88
delphinium 20, 22, 46,
    47, 53, 62, 63, 75,
    84, 85, 159, 160
dill 50, 123, 159, 164
dried flowers 142, 143
    hydrangea balls 128,
        129, 130

E

elderberry 42
eucalyptus 78, 138, 139
euphorbia 84, 85

F

ferns 76, 77
foam (oasis) 92, 122,
    130, 132, 138, 147,
    157, 163, 166-7
foliage 58, 59, 66, 67,
    78, 142, 163, 164-5
    acer 110-11, 112
    camellia 18, 19, 30,
        117, 122, 123
    cotinus 108, 109
    cotoneaster 138, 139
    eucalyptus 138, 139
    in floral foam (oasis)
        166
    in garlands 148
    holly 138, 139
    laurustinus 164
    magnolia 88
    myrtle 164
    in wreaths 132, 142,
        143, 150
foxglove 50, 51, 70, 71,
    158

fritillary 88
snake's head 118, 119
fruit bowls 134

G

garlands 128, 134, 148,
    149
glasses 134
goblets 138, 139
grasses 62, 63
green bells 75, 84, 85,
    144, 145
grouping flowers 159

H

hammers 162
hand-tying 78-9, 163
hat decoration 40-1
heather 62, 63, 135
hellebore
    (Christmas rose) 34,
    35, 72, 73, 120, 121,
    130, 131, 132, 134
herbs 22
holly 126, 138, 139, 140,
    141
honeysuckle 66
hyacinth 24, 65, 158, 162
    grape 25, 26, 27
    'Woodstock' 98, 99
hydrangea 9, 30, 36, 37,
    39, 52, 53, 60, 61, 62,
    63, 69, 70, 75, 78, 79,
    92, 96, 97, 104, 108,
    109, 112, 113, 123, 136,
    137, 142, 143, 150, 158,
    159, 162, 164
    balls 128, 129, 130
    wreaths 132, 133

I

ivy 134, 140, 148

J

Jacob's ladder 46, 47
jardinières 44, 45
jars 45, 57, 72, 73,
    144, 145, 159
jasmine 116, 117, 150,
    151

jugs 22, 24, 25, 26, 27,
36, 37, 46, 47, 65, 66,
[illegible], 96, 108, 109, 112, 113,
163, 164-5

K

knives 157

L

larkspur 159, 164, 165
laurustinus 164
lavender 142, 143
lichen 130, 140
lilac 18, 30, 34, 35,
116, 117, 120, 121,
158, 162, 167
white 130, 131
lily-of-the-valley 44, 45
loose arrangements 163

M

magnolia 34, 35, 39, 88,
89, 136, 137, 158
milk churns 84, 85
mimosa 36, 37
mint 22, 159
molucella 164, 165
monkshood 159
moss 150
muscari
see hyacinth, grape
myrtle 164, 165

N

narcissus 24, 25
paper white 72, 73
New Year 64
nigella 58, 59

O

oasis see foam
orange blossom 46, 47,
58, 59
orchid, slipper 104,
112, 113

P

paint pots 84, 85
pans 64, 65
paper white
see narcissus
peonies 20, 22, 30, 46,
47, 50-1, 158, 159
peppercorns 130, 131,
136, 137, 148, 150
pine 128, 142, 143, 147
in garlands 148, 149
in wreaths 150, 151
pine cones 150
pink 91, 158
poppy 158
Icelandic 92, 93, 98,
99, 104, 116, 117
pots 64, 70, 71, 97
preparing flowers 162
pussy willow 64

R

ranunculus 18, 19, 23,
24, 25, 26, 27, 92, 93,
158, 164
ribbons
for corsages 163
for garlands 148
for table centres 144,
145
for wreaths 138, 139,
140
rose hips 140, 147
rosemary 58, 59, 78,
142, 143
rose 12-22, 30, 32, 34,
35, 36, 37, 46, 47, 52,
53, 96, 97, 114, 115,
158, 159, 167
'Blue Pacific' 16, 17
climbing 20, 22, 66
'Combo' 108, 109
containers for 16, 17,
18, 19, 20, 21, 22, 23,
32-3
'Cool Water' 16, 17
in corsages 41, 48, 49
'Curiosa' 144, 145
'Grand Prix' 144, 145
hand-tying 78-9
'Issy' 144, 145
'Magic Pepito' 16, 17

'Memory Lane' 108, 109
paper 135
piano 138
[illegible] 16, 17, 74
porcelain 22, 23, 49
silk 49
'Sweet Avalanche' 16, 17
in table centres 16,
17, 42, 43, 145
in wreaths 92, 93
'Yves Piaget' 18, 19

S

sage 142, 143
scabious 53, 60, 61, 159
scent 58
bulbs 64, 98
Christmas garlands 128
Christmas wreaths 142
lilac 34
lily-of-the-valley 44
roses 18, 52
sweet peas 52
scissors 67, 157, 162
secateurs 157, 162
sedum 43
snapdragon 84, 85, 159
snowberries 36, 37, 76, 77
Solomon's seal 18, 84, 85
spring flowers 24, 25,
26, 27
statice 92, 108, 109,
144, 145
sterilisation tablets 157
stock 158, 159
stoneware 58, 59
storage caddies 34-5
string 78, 148, 157, 163
sweet pea 50, 53, 106-7,
158, 159, 163

T

table centres 16, 17,
20, 22, 42, 43, 70,
144, 145, 159, 164
tape 122, 157, 163, 166
teapots 130, 131
terracotta 59
tools 156-7, 162
tulip 24, 87, 88, 91,
117, 158, 162, 163
tureens 69, 70

U

urns 50, 117, 122, 123,
138, 139

V

vases 23, 32-3, 39, 40,
45, 47, 51, 52, 53, 60,
61, 86-7, 88, 90, 91,
93, 106-7, 121, 138,
160, 163
veronica 159
vibernum 18, 19, 34, 35,
142, 167

W

water 114
bulbs 72
buying flowers 158
foliage 67
hellebores 100
preparing flowers 162,
164
sterilisation tablets
for 157
urns 116, 122, 139
wreaths 132, 150
waxflower 46, 47, 75,
78, 159
wild flowers 118
winter flowers
see hellebore
wire 59, 122-3, 157, 163
corsages 49, 60
garlands 148
hydrangea balls 130
sweet peas 106, 112
wreaths 142, 150
witch hazel 116, 117
wreaths 150-1
Christmas 132, 133,
135, 138, 139, 140,
142, 143

COPYRIGHT

First published in Great Britain in 2011
by Kyle Books
an imprint of Kyle Cathie Ltd
192–198 Vauxhall Bridge Road
London SW1V 1DX
general.enquiries@kylebooks.com
www.kylebooks.com

10 9 8 7 6 5

ISBN 978-1-85626-971-1

Text © 2011 Vic Brotherson
Photographs © 2011 Catherine Gratwicke
Design © 2011 Kyle Books

Editor: Judith Hannam
Photographer: Catherine Gratwicke
Creative consultant: Kate Dwyer
Designer: Helen Bratby
Production: Sheila Smith and Nic Jones
Copy editor: Catherine Ward
Proof reader: Abi Waters
Indexer: Susan Tricklebank

A Cataloguing in Publication record for this
title is available from the British Library

Printed and bound by C & C Offset Printing

APOLOGIES & APPRECIATION

Firstly I owe my daughter Betsy an apology for rarely being at home when she woke up and for never being able to use my laptop as I was doing 'book stuff', and thanks for the brief 'yup' and 'nah' when asked an opinion. To my husband, Simon, I also owe many 'thank yous' as he has learnt to cook brilliantly, far better than me, meaning I now may have to pretend to be writing a book forever. He was also an extra pair of eyes on pictures, and ears on my evenings tap tapping away. To them both and for them both I am very grateful.

My family – Mum and Dad (Harriet & Peter), two sisters (Em & Charl) their partners (Lee & Justin) and niece and nephew (Agnes & Albert) – have put up with Scarlet & Violet the two honorary family members, so thank you and sorry. C & J let me turn their home upside down and abuse it like my own (IOU flowers).

The Scarlets & Violets to whom I owe massive thanks are my sister Em, for everything I can't do, which is a lot, and her constant encouragement, amazing stash of fabrics, ribbons and everything else you could imagine; Kate Reeves, my right hand and loyal friend; Lucy O'Donnell, my other right hand and continuously happy shop girl; Hannah McIntosh, for her swift fingers and funny tales of going out; Roma Foulds, for her steady hard work and dedication; Gabi Manivit, for all the fiddly bits and delicious cakes; and Anthony Barnell, for putting up with us all and being totally reliable always. I am enormously grateful and owe you all apologies for working you so hard.

I must also thank The Paradise for letting me shoot there. Enormous thanks and gratitude must go to John – to whom I also owe apologies for late night flower texts; Trevor, Paul and Kenny (SR Allen); David (GB foliage); Mick, Bob and Sol (Pratleys); Eddie (Goodchild), John (Bloomfield) and Eric (John Austins); and Terry (Zest) for all the beautiful flowers and foliage pictured in this book. Huge thanks, too, to Jamie, who is my brilliant porter and muscle at the market; without him I would forget to collect half my flowers. New Covent Garden Market makes what I do possible and without it I would struggle.

Finally plentiful thanks must go to Judith Hannam (as my publisher and reality check), Cath Gratwicke (my photographer and delight), Kate Dwyer (a second pair of eyes and hands and prolific emailer) and Helen Bratby (genius designer and joy to work with), all of whom made the whole experience a pleasure. I am so pleased and relieved. Thank you.